red roses
for my love

poetry by
edgar holmes

edgar holmes

red roses for my love

CHAPTERS

edgar holmes

dedicated to my wife. as long
as i write for you, my pen
could never run dry.

red roses for my love

edgar holmes

Chapter One

red roses for my love

The Soil

even
the most beautiful
of flowers
beginning as a seed
will never
bloom
if it is not planted
in loving soil

the problem
with writing
about you

is that
there is nothing
more poetic
in this world
than the wordless way
you look at me
in those small,
small, loving moments

edgar holmes

you give
so much love
to everything
and everyone
on this earth

except yourself.

red roses for my love

i like to think
there have been many times
we have met before
and not realized it

our fairy tale
is too perfect
not to include
some foreshadowing

edgar holmes

often times
the simplest things
in life
and in love
are the most beautiful
singing as a choir
a harmony of one

red roses for my love

edgar holmes

there will always be
those in your life
who want to convince you
that you owe them
a piece of yourself
despite the fact
that they give
nothing
in return

red roses for my love

a cherished smile
the sun shines
and there you are

edgar holmes

there have been
many tears
shed
over the years
over past lovers
who never understood
your true worth

red roses for my love

my darling,
you bring the light
with you
wherever you go

the places that ache with pain
will one day be filled
with a wondrous joy

the places that rain
with sadness
will shine again

do not lose hope
do not despair
life waits for you.

red roses for my love

edgar holmes

some people
will always feel entitled
to your time

never let someone
lay claim
to any part of you
that you do not want
to share

red roses for my love

when i met you
i instantly realized
why some men
claim to see angels
walking about
the earth

edgar holmes

a song i sing
the simple things
my love for you
goes on

in cloudy skies
i realize
the sun
was always you

red roses for my love

i begun to count
the scars
as they added up
on my flesh
over the years

it began to seem
like they would never
fade away

love was the salve
that showed me
there was still
hope

edgar holmes

by the light

of that fire

in your eyes

reflected

love showed me

who

you are.

red roses for my love

edgar holmes

i remember the time
i found
one of your earrings
left at my place

hope struck me
that you
would leave
more and more
of your things
and yourself
here

until eventually
almost by serendipity
the life
i imagined with you
would slowly
become reality

red roses for my love

i have never promised you
anything
but honesty
and so i would never
hide from you
the truth
or the pain

edgar holmes

nothing makes a man
believe in god
quite as quickly
as being blessed
with the woman
of his dreams

red roses for my love

sometimes
new life
comes disguised
as death

do not forget
that the winter
must die
for the new life
of spring
to take root

edgar holmes

as you
blow on your coffee
taking in the smell
i look upon
the mountain peaks
all around
and think

i couldn't have been
more lucky.

red roses for my love

edgar holmes

the paint

        the canvas

    the brush

all my art

leads back to you.

red roses for my love

as statues of angels
come from blocks of granite
you saw in me
a redeeming beauty
i never even saw
myself.

edgar holmes

excitement
isn't the only thing
that matters, you know.

rollercoasters
are fun, once in a while
but i would never want
to live on one.

red roses for my love

your last man
never listened
when you talked to him
about your day at work
or the drama
between co-workers

i always wanted
to make a point
of showing you i care
about even these
smallest of details.

edgar holmes

the waves crash

    do you hear them?

or do they fade into a roar
as they accumulate?

and so i wonder

    in my life

if all i am will be lost
to the noise of humanity

red roses for my love

edgar holmes

Chapter Two

red roses for my love

The Rain

edgar holmes

do not forget

though it is cold
and drenches your clothes
there would be no
beautiful flowers
without the rain

red roses for my love

have you ever bought a
notebook with a beautiful
design
and almost didn't want
to write in it
for fear of ruining it?

loving you
was kind of like that.

edgar holmes

the smell of a candle
greeting you
as you walk through
the door

tonight
will be made
of unforgettable memories

red roses for my love

edgar holmes

even the pain
of being

stuck in traffic

is assuaged
by your lovely presence

red roses for my love

i have never seen
a girl looking so innocent
be so enthralled
with serial killers
and catastrophes

edgar holmes

nervous, stuttering
unsure

new love
can be like that sometimes

red roses for my love

i wish
that i
was a better
singer
so that i
could write you
songs
of love

edgar holmes

it wasn't just about
the sex

there was just something
about the way
she laid there
satisfied
when we were done
that made my heart
melt a little more

red roses for my love

edgar holmes

sorrow proceeds
as if it were invited
to be there
demanding its due
taking the season
as its own

red roses for my love

eyes closed

.. ..

the wind
breezing through my fingers
a peace
a simple, simple peace.

never entertain
the doubts that reach
up towards you
from the depths
below

you are worth loving
you are beautiful
you are worth it.

red roses for my love

fuck the odds
against us

fuck the possibility
of failure

i need you.

edgar holmes

fuck mozart and beethoven
fuck van gogh and rembrant
the most beautiful art
is your face
on the brink
of satisfaction

red roses for my love

edgar holmes

the gentle perfume
of the ocean

the world
at peace
with itself

red roses for my love

even if you fall
even if the rain
threatens to drown you

do not forget
that you
are strong enough
to rise above
the waves

edgar holmes

every
story
has
its
middle

every
book
has
a
spine

red roses for my love

your
story
is
never
over

even
when
life
is
dark

edgar holmes

there is nothing
quite like
the simple pleasure
of enjoying a cocktail
on the beach
with the person
you love most

red roses for my love

all
the things
we ever lost
before this time
will one day find
their way back to us

red roses for my love

think of the effortless way
a freshly planted flower
not needing to be told
grows without a care
and so also it is
with you

edgar holmes

sometimes
even though i have seen it
a million times
i catch a glimpse
of that ring
on your finger
and smile involuntarily

every day
i grow more grateful
that you are mine

red roses for my love

true love
never takes you
for granted

edgar holmes

it is only human
to struggle
with letting go

red roses for my love

y o u .

        (the world turns to slow
                     motion)

d e s i r e .

        (burn my luck, it's
           you or nothing)

edgar holmes

though i love
the convenience
of a smartphone picture

nothing compares
to the raw moment
that comes through
in a polaroid

red roses for my love

nice

edgar holmes

though you pursue
escape
you can never
get away
from the thing
deep within you
that makes you want
to escape

red roses for my love

the strongest branch
is not the one
that holds fast
rigid and unmoving

the strongest branch
is the one
that flows with the wind
flexible, at ease

edgar holmes

i
don't
need
anything
else
on
this
earth
as
long
as
i
have
you
by
my
side

red roses for my love

there is such
an anxiety
between
your
texts

                    the space
          between them is filled
   with my doubts & insecurities

73

edgar holmes

the true test of trust in a
relationship is not the
vulnerability of leaving your
phone unlocked around them

the true test of trust in a
relationship is being alone
with their unlocked phone and
not looking through it.

red roses for my love

edgar holmes

existential crisis looms
questions
of what it means
to live life

suddenly you
pull me back
from the edge

you make everything
real
no matter how
disoriented
i feel

red roses for my love

i was never too good
at mathematics
i found it confusing
and unhelpful

but you did it
so effortlessly
and even though
i once despised it
entirely;

even math
reflecting
a piece of you
is beautiful
somehow

edgar holmes

you are loved
 you are loved
  you are loved
   you are loved
    you are loved
     you are loved
      you are loved
       you are loved
        you are loved
         you are loved
          you are loved
           you are loved
            you are loved
             you are loved
              you are loved
               you are loved
                you are loved
                 you are loved

red roses for my love

once upon a time
there was a man
who didn't yet
know himself

but the moment
you entered his life
suddenly everything
made sense

Chapter Three

red roses for my love

The Sun

edgar holmes

it's okay
for your dreams
to change

it's okay
for what you want
to change

do not be afraid
of the changes
of life

because that's
what makes it
life

red roses for my love

i never knew
what it was
about seeing you
smoking a joint
off our hotel balcony
in hawaii, at night
the stars in full view

i never knew
exactly what about
seeing you do this
was so sexy
to me

reaching around
with my hands
groping
in the dark
not seeing
where i wanted
to go

i was lost

you
were the light
that showed me
the way

red roses for my love

edgar holmes

you and i
were pulled together
irresistibly
and oh so naturally

magnetic
the way
we fit together

red roses for my love

take your burdens
those heavy rocks
from your shoulders

lay them down
at your feet
for just a moment

breathe in
and out
slowly

you deserve
to feel the peace
of this moment

bravery
does not prevent
fear

bravery
emerges from fear
speaking out
declaring
you will not be moved

red roses for my love

i wish that i
could watch
the dreams you dream
in the night

i wish that i
could come along with you
and fly among
galaxies and aliens
with your innermost spirit

edgar holmes

i love thinking back
to those moments

two college kids
not knowing
a goddamn thing
but thinking
we knew
what life
was all about

smoking away the days

oh what a ways we have come
from then

red roses for my love

edgar holmes

just because
your life
includes sad chapters
doesn't mean
it's a bad one

the lovelies stories
are composed of ups and downs
of challenges and trials

your story
though it may
include sad chapters
will have
the happy ending
you always wanted

red roses for my love

the simplest days
spent inside
with you
watching netflix
and just relaxing

the simplest days
with you
the simplicity
of us

immeasurably beautiful.

edgar holmes

everything passes
eventually

do not forget
that even
the longest night
will eventually
give way
to sunlight

red roses for my love

i am obsessed with you.

i didn't want to say it
to freak you out
or scare you

but i must
tell you
the truth

i am obsessed
with you.

edgar holmes

you are a rosebud
there is immeasurable beauty
waiting
within you

even if you can't see it
just yet.

red roses for my love

edgar holmes

life
before you
was dark
and dead

you were the sun
that rose up
upon my life

red roses for my love

laughing
and smiling
like typical tourists
happily taking pictures
on vacation

i didn't mind
looking like a fool

i guess that's
just something that happens
when you fall
in love

edgar holmes

there are still
so many stories
so many truths
still left
to be uncovered

red roses for my love

do not be afraid
of letting go
of comfortable ideas
or ways of acting
that you have

let go
of your preconceptions
and try to find
the real truth

edgar holmes

i remember
every rose
i have given you
they were each
special
in their own ways

red roses for my love

edgar holmes

the cosmos
is as much
within us
as it is
out there
in the night's sky

red roses for my love

to know oneself
is as impossible
as holding sand
in the wind

edgar holmes

the future
is not
set in stone

do not lose hope
there is still
so much left
to live for

as long
as i
have you

i will
always
have
enough

edgar holmes

i made a wish
i wished for you
on the breeze
the seedlings blew

red roses for my love

edgar holmes

your love
makes even
the most mundane things
feel
like a miracle

distance
is not an excuse
to get away
with things

distance
is an opportunity
to prove your loyalty
to each other

edgar holmes

i had been feeling down
for some time
as winter had
its hold on me

but on that day
i finally felt
the precious light
of the sun

and smiled, for the first time
in a long time.

red roses for my love

love
does not tame you

love
makes you feel

wild
and free

simple moments
with you
doing everything
we were taught
never to do

red roses for my love

Chapter Four

red roses for my love

My Lovely Rose

edgar holmes

i want
to slowly become
more and more
like you

red roses for my love

she was the feeling of a
midsummer night, the freedom
racing through my veins as i
fall in love with you

edgar holmes

watching you
engrossed in a book
sipping your tea

i've never been
more in love

red roses for my love

edgar holmes

love people
for who
they are,

not just
what they do
for you.

red roses for my love

i ponder
the mysteries
of the stars

wondering
what they know
that i
could never grasp

edgar holmes

never forget -

love
is supposed
to make you feel

good

about yourself.

red roses for my love

reuniting
with an old friend
is like
finding a twenty dollar bill
in the pocket
of a jacket
you haven't worn
in a while

edgar holmes

i traced my hand
along the glass
feeling the cold chill
of the outside air
held back
by this thin sheet

i smiled
breathing in
the petrichor

red roses for my love

edgar holmes

be patient
with yourself

learning self love
can be
a long
and difficult
process

red roses for my love

don't just hear her
when she speaks

listen.

edgar holmes

do not forget
that even though
it doesn't seem like it
sometimes

there are still
good people
left
in this dark world

red roses for my love

as long as you love each other
fearlessly, unafraid to be
tested and to fight for what
you have, everything will turn
out okay.

edgar holmes

we had only been dating
two weeks at the time

you suggested we go
skinny dipping
down by the beach

as i saw you
getting in
to the water

i realized
you were so, so
out of my league

red roses for my love

edgar holmes

no matter the temptations
you will always be
the only one
i want

red roses for my love

we
were destined
for one another

there is no
doubt
in my mind

edgar holmes

you are strong enough
for the life
you live

red roses for my love

everyone else
is just a shadow
of the real thing

you
are the only one
who matters

she loves me
she loves me not
the petals
fall to the floor

red roses for my love

edgar holmes

your strength
to overcome
every difficulty
is so much
greater
than you know

red roses for my love

being with you
isn't just about
not being alone

it's so much more
than that

being with you
brings out
the best
in me

you
are so full of giving
so willing
to be a good person

but there is a limit
to how much
you can give
just as you cannot
give too much blood
without dying

red roses for my love

toxic people will eat away at
the fabric of your soul; they
will corrode even the shiniest
surface into rust.

edgar holmes

the joyous moment
a caterpillar
turns into
a butterfly

you will have this moment
too
one day

red roses for my love

edgar holmes

do not let anyone
enter your life
who believes
that treating you
with the respect
and loyalty
you deserve
is merely
optional

red roses for my love

you are such a lovely person
glowing with love
some people just want
to sit in your light
and soak it up
without ever giving
anything back

edgar holmes

you may feel
like you
are nothing special

but one day
the one for you
will look at you
and see
everything
they were waiting
all their life for

red roses for my love

be forgiving
but not a pushover
be strong
but not arrogant
be loving
but keep your standards

edgar holmes

her eyes—

you could spend a lifetime
looking into those eyes
and never run out
of new details
to fall in love with

red roses for my love

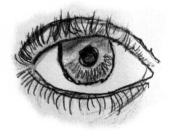

edgar holmes

as long as i am alive you will
always have fresh flowers on
your dresser to greet you when
you get home

red roses for my love

rose petals were your path from the front door, the room dark and quiet save for the gentle glow of candlelight and light music in the background. you followed the path, a smile tugging at the corners of your lips. a bath filled with bubbles, a glass of wine at the ready for you.

i would do anything to make your day better, to help you feel like the world isn't quite so burdensome as it feels sometimes. i want to lift the weight from your shoulders and let you rest.

i love you, my darling.

edgar holmes

red roses for my love

thank you so much for reading my third poetry collection. i feel that this is my most personal collection to date, and i hope that even though it is so personal to me, you will still find some of yourself in these pages as well.

never give up on love, my friends. never give up on your dreams of being loved for exactly who you are, by a partner who loves and truly understands you. never give up on this life.

all my love,

-edgar holmes

p. s.

you can find me on instagram @edgarholmespoetry

Made in the USA
Monee, IL
15 December 2019

18690702R00090